T0011152

Say No to Plastic Waste

Plastic

This is plastic.

This is plastic.

This is plastic too!

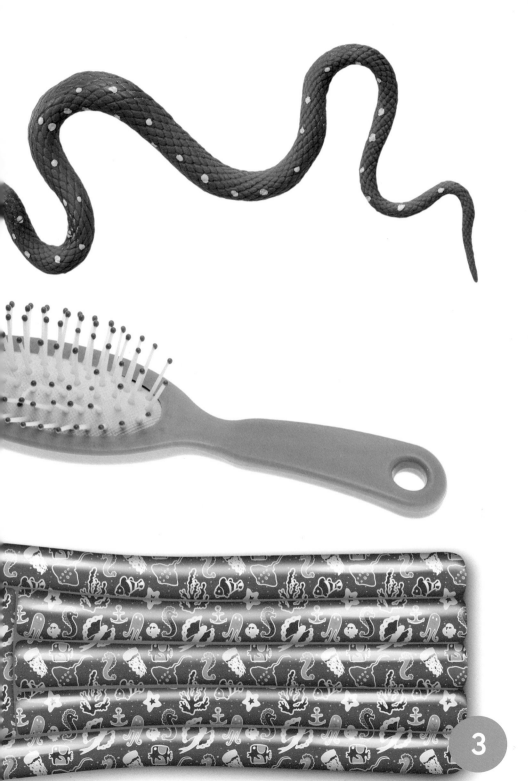

We need plastic

My helmet is made from plastic. My helmet will keep me safe.

Look at the **fort**.
The fort is made from
plastic. I am safe
in the fort.

Plastic pollution

Some plastic is not good for the **environment**.

This plastic is in the water.
The fish will think
it is food.

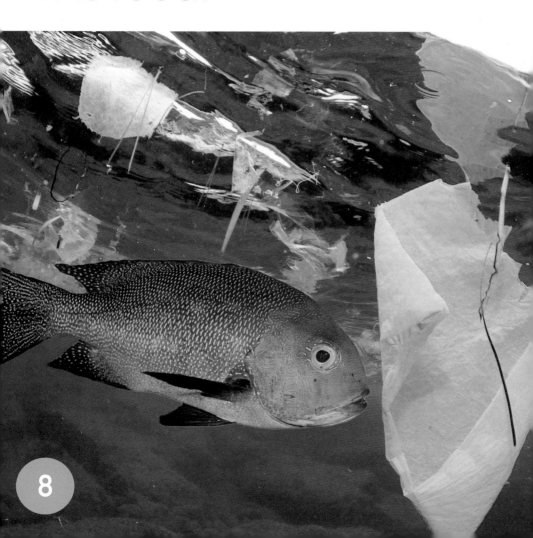

The bird will think
this plastic is food too!
It will try to eat it.

No to plastic

We can say no to plastic.

This is my lunch bag.
It is made from paper.

Look at our shopping bag.

It is made from cotton.

Recycling plastic

We can help to **recycle** plastic at home.
We put our
plastic bottles in here.

Glossary

 environment

 fort

 recycle